McKinney

by Iain Gray

Lang**Syne**

PUBLISHING

WRITING *to* REMEMBER

79 Main Street, Newtongrange,
Midlothian EH22 4NA
Tel: 0131 344 0414
E-mail: info@lang-syne.co.uk
www.langsyneshop.co.uk

Design by Dorothy Meikle
Printed by Printwell Ltd
© Lang Syne Publishers Ltd 2023

All rights reserved. No part of this publication may be reproduced, stored or introduced into a retrieval system, or transmitted in any form or by any means (electronic, mechanical, photocopying, recording or otherwise) without the prior written permission of Lang Syne Publishers Ltd.

ISBN 978-1-85217-766-9

McKinney

MOTTOES include:
Fortune favours the bold *(MacKinnon)*
I shine not burn *(Mackenzie)*

CRESTS include:
A boar's head with a shin bone
in its mouth *(MacKinnon)*
A mount in flames *(Mackenzie)*

TERRITORIES include:
Mull, Skye, Kintail, Ross-shire

NAME variations include:
MacCammie
MacKimmie
McKimmie
MacKinney
McShimmie
MacKimmey

Chapter one:

The origins of the clan system

by Rennie McOwan

The original Scottish clans of the Highlands and the great families of the Lowlands and Borders were gatherings of families, relatives, allies and neighbours for mutual protection against rivals or invaders.

Scotland experienced invasion from the Vikings, the Romans and English armies from the south. The Norman invasion of what is now England also had an influence on land-holding in Scotland. Some of these invaders stayed on and in time became 'Scottish'.

The word clan derives from the Gaelic language term 'clann', meaning children, and it was first used many centuries ago as communities were formed around tribal lands in glens and mountain fastnesses.

The format of clans changed over the centuries, but at its best the chief and his family held the land on behalf of all, like trustees, and the ordinary clansmen and women believed they had a blood relationship with the founder of their clan.

There were two way duties and obligations. An inadequate chief could be deposed and replaced by someone of greater ability.

Clan people had an immense pride in race. Their relationship with the chief was like adult children to a father and they had a real dignity.

The concept of clanship is very old and a more feudal notion of authority gradually crept in.

Pictland, for instance, was divided into seven principalities ruled by feudal leaders who were the strongest and most charismatic leaders of their particular groups.

By the sixth century the 'British' kingdoms of Strathclyde, Lothian and Celtic Dalriada (Argyll) had emerged and Scotland, as one nation, began to take shape in the time of King Kenneth MacAlpin.

Some chiefs claimed descent from ancient kings which may not have been accurate in every case.

By the twelfth and thirteenth centuries the clans and families were more strongly brought under the central control of Scottish monarchs.

Lands were awarded and administered more and more under royal favour, yet the power of the area clan chiefs was still very great.

The long wars to ensure Scotland's

independence against the expansionist ideas of English monarchs extended the influence of some clans and reduced the lands of others.

Those who supported Scotland's greatest king, Robert the Bruce, were awarded the territories of the families who had opposed his claim to the Scottish throne.

In the Scottish Borders country – the notorious Debatable Lands – the great families built up a ferocious reputation for providing warlike men accustomed to raiding into England and occasionally fighting one another.

Chiefs had the power to dispense justice and to confiscate lands and clan warfare produced a society where martial virtues – courage, hardiness, tenacity – were greatly admired.

Gradually the relationship between the clans and the Crown became strained as Scottish monarchs became more orientated to life in the Lowlands and, on occasion, towards England.

The Highland clans spoke a different language, Gaelic, whereas the language of Lowland Scotland and the court was Scots and in more modern times, English.

Highlanders dressed differently, had different

customs, and their wild mountain land sometimes seemed almost foreign to people living in the Lowlands.

It must be emphasised that Gaelic culture was very rich and story-telling, poetry, piping, the clarsach (harp) and other music all flourished and were greatly respected.

Highland culture was different from other parts of Scotland but it was not inferior or less sophisticated.

Central Government, whether in London or Edinburgh, sometimes saw the Gaelic clans as a challenge to their authority and some sent expeditions into the Highlands and west to crush the power of the Lords of the Isles.

Nevertheless, when the eighteenth century Jacobite Risings came along the cause of the Stuarts was mainly supported by Highland clans.

The word Jacobite comes from the Latin for James – Jacobus. The Jacobites wanted to restore the exiled Stuarts to the throne of Britain.

The monarchies of Scotland and England became one in 1603 when King James VI of Scotland (1st of England) gained the English throne after Queen Elizabeth died.

The Union of Parliaments of Scotland and England, the Treaty of Union, took place in 1707.

Some Highland clans, of course, and Lowland families opposed the Jacobites and supported the incoming Hanoverians.

After the Jacobite cause finally went down at Culloden in 1746 a kind of ethnic cleansing took place. The power of the chiefs was curtailed. Tartan and the pipes were banned in law.

Many emigrated, some because they wanted to, some because they were evicted by force. In addition, many Highlanders left for the cities of the south to seek work.

Many of the clan lands became home to sheep and deer shooting estates.

But the warlike traditions of the clans and the great Lowland and Border families lived on, with their descendants fighting bravely for freedom in two world wars.

Remember the men from whence you came, says the Gaelic proverb, and to that could be added the role of many heroic women.

The spirit of the clan, of having roots, whether Highland or Lowland, means much to thousands of people.

Meanwhile, many families proudly boast the heraldic device known as a Coat of Arms,.

The central motif of the Coat of Arms would originally have been what was sometimes borne on the shield of a warrior to distinguish himself from others on the battlefield.

Clan warfare produced a society where courage and tenacity were greatly admired

Chapter two:

Sprung from fire

A name of fiery roots, 'McKinney' and its spelling variants including 'MacKinney', stems from the Scottish Gaelic *MacCionaodha*, with 'Mc/Mac' indicating 'son of' and 'cion' a personal name denoting 'affection' or 'respect.'

'Aodh', meanwhile, refers to the Celtic fire god of the name, hence *Mac Cionaodha* denotes 'son of the beloved of Aodh' or, in a much shorter descriptive form, 'firesprung.'

With similar connotations, the Irish Gaelic form of McKinney/MacKinney is *Mac Cionaoith*, a tribal grouping who once flourished as Lord of Truagh in what is now Co. Monaghan.

In the Highlands and Islands of Scotland, the McKinneys/MacKinneys were a sept, or sub-branch, of two noted clans – Clan MacKinnon and Clan Mackenzie.

Derived from the Gaelic *clanna*, meaning 'children', a clan was a close-knit tribal grouping settled in a particular territory and whose members – or 'children', or 'kin' – owed unswerving loyalty to a chief who, in turn, was bound by duty and honour to protect them.

Not all members of a clan, such as the Mckinneys, necessarily shared the same surname as the chief – known as *ceann-cinnidh*, meaning 'head and chief of the family' – and these 'kindred of the clan', or 'kinsfolk', were recognised, as they are to this day, as septs of the clan.

As such, they are entitled to share in the clan's heritage and traditions that include the right to display its tartan and heraldry of crest and motto – this heraldry recognised by the Lord Lyon King of Arms of Scotland, the final arbiter on all matters heraldic.

In the case of the McKinneys/MacKinneys, they share the Clan MacKinnon motto 'Fortune favours the bold' and crest of a boar's head with a shin bone in its mouth, and the Mackenzie motto 'I shine not burn' and crest of a mount in flames.

The rather unusual Clan MacKinnon crest is based on a legend concerning one of their early chiefs who sought overnight shelter in a cave after becoming separated from a hunting party on the shores of Loch Scavaig, on the Isle of Skye.

Having prepared some venison to cook over

a fire, he was suddenly attacked by a ferocious wild boar that had charged into the cave.

The quick-thinking chief rammed the deer's leg he had butchered into the boar's mouth, jamming it open, and then killing it – the incident subsequently proudly commemorated in his crest.

The Gaelic form of MacKinnon is *Mac Fhionghuin*, derived from a personal name denoting 'fair son' or 'fair born' and, in the form 'Finguni', is held to indicate descent from a Bishop of Iona of the name.

Other authorities also note the clan can trace an ancestry back to *Cinéad mac Ailpìn*, or 'Alpin', of the *Dál Riata*, or Dalriada, the ancient kingdom that included parts of Scotland and Ireland.

In common with Clan Gregor, or MacGregor, the MacKinnons are therefore held to be of the royal *Siol Alpin* – the 'race' or 'seed' of Alpin.

The Mackenzies trace their descent from a twelfth century chief, while their name is an Anglicisation of the Gaelic personal name *Coinneach*, denoting 'handsome', or 'comely.'

By 1297 they had established the iconic Eilean Donan Castle, sited on a tidal island where the sea lochs of Loch Alsh, Loch Duich and Loch Long meet, as their stronghold.

As kindred of the MacKinnons and the Mackenzies, the McKinneys/MacKinneys shared in both their glorious fortunes and tragic misfortunes.

In common with other clans, not only in Scotland but also Ireland, the MacKinnons and Mackenzies were frequently embroiled in internecine and bloody clan warfare – with Clan Maclean one of the main MacKinnon foes, and the Earls of Ross and their allies the main rivals of the Mackenzies.

But differences were set aside when called on to rally to the cause of Scotland's freedom and independence, and the McKinneys/MacKinneys as kindred of the MacKinnons and the Mackenzies played a prominent role in the bitter and bloody Wars of Independence with England.

Scotland was thrown into crisis in 1286 with the death of King Alexander II and the death four years later of his successor, the Maid of Norway, who died while en route to Scotland to take up the crown.

John Balliol was controversially enthroned at Scone as King of Scots in 1292 – but fatefully for the nation they had asked the powerful King Edward I – known as the Hammer of the Scots – to arbitrate in the bitter dispute over the succession to the throne, and the hapless Balliol found himself Edward's chosen man.

The Scots rose in revolt against the imperialist designs of Edward in July of 1296 but the ruthless monarch brought the entire nation under his subjugation little less than a month later, garrisoning strategic locations throughout the length and breadth of the nation, and demanding the signing of the *Ragman Roll*.

Known as the *Ragman Roll* because of the profusion of ribbons that dangle from the seals of the signatories, it was a humiliating treaty of fealty to the conquering Edward that was signed at Berwick by 1,500 Scottish earls, bishops and burgesses.

But subjugation under the iron fist of English occupation did not sit well with the proud Scots and the great patriot William Wallace raised the banner of revolt in May of 1297.

A charismatic leader and an expert in the tactics of guerrilla warfare, Wallace and his hardened band of freedom fighters set Scotland aflame – boosting the morale of their fellow countrymen as they inflicted a stunning series of defeats on the English garrisons.

This culminated in the liberation of practically all of Scotland following the battle of Stirling Bridge, on September 11, 1297.

But, defeated at the battle of Falkirk on July 22, 1298, after earlier being appointed Guardian of Scotland, Sir William Wallace was eventually betrayed and captured seven years later, and brutally executed in London as a 'traitor' on August 23, 1305.

His execution only served to further inflame Scottish patriotism, however, and the cause of the nation's freedom was taken up again, this time under the inspired leadership of the great warrior king Robert the Bruce, who had been enthroned as king at Scone in March of 1306.

Over the next eight long years, Bruce was supported by a band of loyal supporters such as the MacKinnons and Mackenzies and their kinsfolk including the McKinneys/MacKinneys.

During these years, it was the MacKinnons who gave him shelter while being pursued through his native Carrick, in Ayrshire, and were rewarded with land on the Isle of Skye following Bruce's great victory at the battle of Bannockburn in 1314, while the Mackenzies also fought in his ranks.

By the summer of 1314, the strategically important and mighty bastion of Stirling Castle was still in English hands, under the command of Sir Philip de Mowbray.

Bruce's brother, Edward, had agreed to a pledge by Mowbray that if the castle was not relieved by battle by midsummer of the following year, then he would surrender.

This made battle inevitable, and by June 23 of 1314 the two armies faced one another at Bannockburn, in sight of the castle.

It was on this day that Bruce killed the English knight Sir Henry de Bohun in single combat, but the battle proper was not fought until the following day, shortly after the rise of the midsummer sun.

The English cavalry launched a desperate but futile charge on the densely packed ranks of Scottish spearmen known as schiltrons, and by the time the sun had sank slowly in the west the English army had been totally routed, with Edward himself only narrowly managing to make his escape from the carnage of the battlefield.

A Scottish army had defeated a 20,000-strong English army under King Edward II less than half this strength, and Scotland's independence had been secured thanks to loyal clans such as the MacKinnons, the Mackenzies and their kinsfolk, the McKinneys.

Chapter three:

Civil wars

As the centuries progressed, there was no escape from the clash and clamour of the battlefield, with Sir John Mackenzie, 9th of Kintail, on the field at the disastrous battle of Flodden on September 9, 1513 – when 5,000 Scots were killed, including James IV, an archbishop, two bishops, eleven earls, fifteen barons and 300 knights.

The Scottish monarch had embarked on the venture after Queen Anne of France, under the terms of the Auld Alliance between Scotland and her nation, appealed to him to 'break a lance' on her behalf and act as her chosen knight.

Crossing the border into England at the head of a 25,000-strong army that included 7,500 clansmen and their kinsmen, James engaged a 20,000-strong force commanded by the Earl of Surrey – but despite their numerical advantage and bravery the Scots

proved no match for the skilled English artillery and superior military tactics of Surrey.

Nearly 35 years later, Mackenzie led his clan at the battle of Pinkie, fought on September 10, 1547, near Musselburgh, in East Lothian, when a 25,000-strong English army under the Duke of Somerset decisively defeated a 35,000-strong Scots army under the Earl of Arran.

Also known as the battle of Pinkie Cleugh, it was fought during the 'Rough Wooing', an attempt by England's dynastically ambitious Henry VIII to force upon the Scots agreement for the future marriage of his infant son Edward to the infant Mary, Queen of Scots.

Despite their superior numbers, what led to the defeat of the Scots in what became known as 'Black Saturday' was that Somerset was backed by a fleet of naval guns at the mouth of the River Esk, and the early loss in the battle of the Scots cavalry after it launched a premature and wild charge on the massed and disciplined English ranks.

Sir John Mackenzie was captured and ransomed – the ransom being paid in the form of a number of cows – but many of his clansmen and kinsfolk were among the massed piles of dead.

Just over twenty years later, the Mackenzies were among a group of nine earls, nine bishops, 18 lairds and others who signed a bond declaring their support for Mary, Queen of Scots after she had been forced to abdicate in favour of her son, James VI (James I of England), by a body known as the Confederate Lords.

On May 23, 1568, Mary's forces, under the command of the Earl of Argyll, had been en route to the mighty bastion of Dumbarton Castle, atop its near inaccessible eminence on Dumbarton Rock, on the Clyde, when it was intercepted by a numerically inferior but tactically superior force led by her half-brother, the Earl of Moray.

Cannon fire had been exchanged before a group of Argyll's infantry tried to force a passage through to the village of Langside, near Glasgow, but they were fired on by a disciplined body of musketeers and had to retreat as Moray launched a cavalry charge on their confused ranks.

The battle proved disastrous for Mary and signalled the death knell of her cause, with more than 100 of her supporters killed or captured and Mary forced to flee into what she then naively thought would be the protection of England's Queen Elizabeth.

But she was instead fated for confinement in a succession of strongholds before her execution on February 8, 1587, in the Great Hall of Fotheringhay Castle, in Northamptonshire.

During the seventeenth century Wars of the Three Kingdoms of Scotland, England and Ireland, the MacKinnons and the Mackenzies at times found themselves fighting on opposite sides.

The conflict in Scotland – essentially a war between Crown and Covenant – had origins in the widely unpopular attempt by King Charles I to impose uniform religious practice between the Church of England and the proudly independent Scottish Kirk, through the introduction into Scotland of the *Episcopal Book of Common Prayer*.

A momentous event occurred on February 28, 1638, with the signing of the National Covenant – a document as important to Scottish history as the equally famed Declaration of Arbroath of 1320.

Described as 'the glorious marriage day of the kingdom with God', the Covenant renounced Roman Catholic belief, pledged to uphold the Presbyterian religion and called for free parliaments and assemblies.

First signed at Edinburgh's Greyfriars Kirk

by nobles, barons, burgesses and ministers, it was subscribed to the following day by hundreds of common folk.

Copies were made and dispatched around the nation and subscribed to by thousands more – with its adherents becoming known as Covenanters.

This led to a civil war that raged between Covenanters and Royalists in Scotland from 1638 until 1649, when Charles I was beheaded on the orders of the English Parliament – whose military arm was the New Model Army under Oliver Cromwell.

The Royalist force was commanded in Scotland by the charismatic James Graham, 1st Marquis of Montrose, and fighting under him were the MacKinnons and their kinsfolk such as the McKinneys/MacKinneys

Although Montrose had initially supported the Covenant, his conscience later dictated that he switch sides, with his great campaigns from 1644 to 1645 known as The Year of Miracles because of his brilliant military successes.

At the battle of Inverlochy, on the west coast, on February 2, 1645 the Earl of Argyll was forced to ignominiously flee in his galley after 1,500 of his Covenanters were wiped out in a surprise attack.

What made Montrose's victory all the more impressive was that his hardy forces had arrived at Inverlochy after an exhausting 36-hour march through knee-deep snow from the area of present-day Fort Augustus.

Another great victory came at the battle of Kilsyth on August 15 then there was defeat at Philiphaugh, near Selkirk, less than a month later.

Montrose, following another defeat at the battle of Carbisdale, Ross-shire, on April 27, 1650 was finally captured after being betrayed. He was hanged a few weeks later, beheaded and his body cut into quarters.

Created Earl of Seaforth in 1623, the Mackenzie chief Colin Mackenzie fought for the Covenanters and led a force that was defeated by Montrose at the battle of Auldearn, but in 1649, following the execution of Charles I, he fought for the Royalist cause of Charles II.

Also fighting for Charles II, Lauchlan MacKinnon, Chief of Clan MacKinnon, raised a regiment that fought on his behalf on September 3, 1651 at the battle of Worcester.

Crushed by Cromwell's New Model Army, about 3,000 Royalists were killed –while up to 8,000

Scottish prisoners were deported to the West Indies, Bermuda and New England to work as indentured labourers.

In the aftermath of the battle, Charles II famously had to hide from his pursuers for a time in the branches of the 'royal oak' at Boscobel, Shropshire; escaping to the Continent, he returned to England on the Restoration of 1660.

Still on the battlefield, the MacKinnons fought as Jacobites – whose cause was the restoration to the throne of the exiled Royal House of Stuart – in both the 1715 and 1745 Risings, with the clan providing shelter for a time to Bonnie Prince Charlie in the aftermath of defeat at the battle of Culloden.

During the 1715 Rising, William Mackenzie, 5th Earl of Seaforth and Chief of Clan Mackenzie, rallied in support of the Jacobites.

But the clan was divided during the 1745 Rising, with Kenneth Mackenzie, Lord Fortrose, raising a number of Independent Highland Companies to support the government, while his cousin George Mackenzie, 3rd Earl of Cromartie, fought as a Jacobite.

Chapter four:

On the world stage

From the stage and music to sport, bearers of the McKinney name have gained recognition at an international level.

On screen, **Bill McKinney** was the American character actor noted for his role in the 1972 film *Deliverance* and roles in a number of Clint Eastwood films.

Born in 1931 in Chattanooga, Tennessee, his first film credit was the 1967 *She Freaks*, while early television credits include *Alias Smith and Jones* and *The Monkees*.

But his major breakthrough on the big screen was *Deliverance*, in the role of a sadistic mountain man, while further acclaim came through roles in Clint Eastwood films including the 1976 *The Outlaw Josey Wales*, the 1974 *Thunderbolt and Lightfoot*, the 1978 *Every Which Way But Loose* and, from 1989, *Pink Cadillac*.

He died in 2011, with further credits including the 1990 *Back to the Future Part III* and the 1999 *The Green Mile* and television credits including *The A-Team* and *The Young Indiana Jones Chronicles*.

An actress and singer among the first to break down some of the barriers that hindered the careers of Africa-Americans in Hollywood, **Nina Mae McKinney** was born in 1912 in Lansing, South Carolina, later moving to New York City.

She made her Broadway debut in 1928 in the chorus line of the hit musical *Blackbirds* and, spotted by the legendary film director King Vidor, she was cast in a starring role in his 1929 *Hallelujah!* – making her the first African-American actress to be cast in a major role in a mainstream film production.

Later signing a five-year contract with MGM, she became the first African-American actor to sign a long-term contract with a major studio.

But discrimination nevertheless still existed in Hollywood and, in common with many of her peers, she made her way to Europe where it was rather less prevalent in the entertainment industry.

While there she was dubbed the 'Black Garbo' because of her stunning good looks. Settling for a time on British shores, Nina had a starring role along with fellow Black-American star Paul Robeson in the 1935 *Sanders of the River*, directed by Alexander Korda.

Another 'first' for the actress was as the first African-American to appear on British television – given her own show in which she showcased her singing talent, in 1936.

Returning to Hollywood, later film credits include the 1939 *Devil's Daughter* and, from 1944, *Dark Waters*.

Back on stage for the final time in 1951 in a production of *Rain*, she died in 1967 and, in 1978, received a posthumous Lifetime Achievement Award from the Black Filmmakers Hall of Fame.

On Irish shores, **Joe McKinney** is the stage, television and film actor and voice-over artist born in 1967 in Rathfarnham, Dublin.

Having worked in his native city on productions including Brendan Behan's *Borstal Boy* (1995) and *An Image for the Rose* (2006), he has appeared in short films including the 2007 *Nuts* and feature films that include the 2004 *Starfish* and, from 2010, an adaptation of *A Christmas Carol*.

From Ireland to Canada, **Mark McKinney** is the comedian and actor born in Ontario in 1959.

Best known for his work with the comedy sketch troupe *The Kids in the Hall*, a cast member from 1995 to 1997 on *Saturday Night Live* and the co-creator of the television series *Slings & Arrows*, his big screen credits include the 1996 *Brain Candy*.

Known for his role of Jason Stillwell in the 1986 martial arts film *No Retreat, No Surrender*, also starring Jean-Claude Van Damme, **Kurt McKinney** is the American film and television actor born in 1962 in Louisville, Kentucky.

Winner of the 1990 Soap Opera Digest Award for Outstanding Male Newcomer: Daytime for his role of Ned Ashton in *General Hospital*, his other television credits include the soap *Guiding Light*.

In the medium of social media, **Charlotte McKinney** is the Instagram personality, actress and model born in 1993 in Orlando, Florida, and whose screen credits include the 2017 film adaptation of television's *Baywatch* and the 2017 remake of *Flatliners*.

Bearers of the McKinney name have displayed particular aptitude in the highly competitive world of sport.

Taking to the ski slopes, **Steve McKinney** was the American Alpine skier and mountaineer recognised as an early pioneer of extreme skiing.

Born in 1953 in Baltimore, Maryland, in 1978 at Portillo, Chile, he became the first speed skier to break the 200km/hr barrier with a run of 200.22km/hr (124.37mph).

Setting seven world speed records between 1974 and 1987, as a mountaineer he led an expedition to Mount Everest in 1986 and, in true daredevil style, became the first person to fly a hang-glider off the formidable mountain.

He was killed in a road accident in November of 1990 when driving to a business meeting in San Francisco. His car is thought to have developed mechanical problems and, pulling off the highway near Sacramento, he apparently clambered into the back seat to sleep before summoning help.
Another vehicle then veered off the road and slammed into the back of his, killing him.

Steve McKinney was the half-brother of the former World Cup Alpine ski racer **Tamara McKinney**, born in 1962 in Lexington, Kentucky.

Winner of four World Cup season titles in 1981 and 1983, Slalom in 1984 and world champion in the combined event in 1989, she is an inductee of the Kentucky Athletic Hall of Fame.

On the basketball court, **John McKinney** was the coach responsible for a number of innovations to the game.

Born in 1935 in Chester, Pennsylvania and head coach for a time in the National Basketball Association (NBA) with the Los Angeles Lakers, he introduced the up-tempo style of play known as 'Showtime.'

His playing career ending following a bicycle accident and named NBA Coach of the Year in 1981 while working with the Kansas City Kings – now the Sacramento Kings – he died in 2018.

In rugby union and rugby league, **Thomas McKinney** was the Northern Irish player who played in both disciplines throughout the 1940s and 1950s.

Born in Ballymena in 1926 and having played at club level rugby union for Scottish team Jed-Forest and representative level rugby league for teams including Great Britain, British Empire XIII and Combined Nationalities, he died in 1999 while, in 2004, he was one of six players inducted into Rugby League Ireland's inaugural Hall of Fame.

From the rugby pitch to the boxing ring, **Kennedy McKinney**, born in 1966 in Hernando Mississippi is the American former boxer who won the bantamweight gold medal at the 1988 Olympics.

Taking up boxing after serving in the U.S. Army and known in the ring as "King", he also won the International Boxing federation (IBF) and World Boxing Organisation (WBO) super bantamweight titles.

In the swimming pool, **Frank McKinney Jr.** was the American champion swimmer who pioneered modern backstroke techniques such as the 'bent-arm' backstroke.

Born in 1938 in Indianapolis, Indiana, he was aged only 16 when he won a gold medal in the 100-meter backstroke at the Pan American Games.

Killed in an air accident in 1992, he was also the recipient of other medals including silver at the 1960 Olympics in the 100-meter backstroke and a gold as part of the U.S. team in the 4x100-meter medley relay.

He was the son of the baseball team co-owner and politician **Frank McKinney Sr.** born in Indianapolis in 1904.

Chairman of the Democratic National Committee from 1951 to 1952 and a delegate from Indiana to a number of Democratic National Conventions, baseball teams he co-owned include the Indianapolis Indians and Pittsburgh Pirates.

A banker by profession and appointed U.S. Ambassador to Spain in 1968, he died in 1974.

In the sport of archery, **Rick McKinney** is the champion American archer born in 1953 in

Decatur, Indiana. Winner of a silver medal at the 1984 Olympics and in the team event at the 1988 Games, he also won the individual title three times and the team title five times between 1975 and 1995 in the World Archery Championships.

From sport to music and, in particular, the gospel genre, Baylus Benjamin McKinney was the American gospel singer, songwriter, music editor and teacher better known as **B.B. McKinney**, born in 1886 in Heflin, Louisiana. The composer of nearly 150 hymns and gospel songs including *Speak to My Heart* and *Wherever He Leads* and an inductee of the Gospel Music Hall of Fame, he died in 1952.

With the popular spelling variant 'McKinnie', **Eric "Ricky" McKinnie** is the blind American gospel singer, songwriter and radio show host who performs with the Grammy Award-winning band Blind Boys of Alabama.

Born in 1952 in Atlanta, Georgia and founder of the group the Ricky McKinnie Singers and having lost his sight when he was aged 23, he is a champion of a number of causes including the Glaucoma Foundation.

From music to the American landscape, **Collin McKinney,** born in 1766 in Hunterdon County,

New Jersey was the land surveyor, merchant and politician who lends his name to both a county and a town in Texas.

The county seat of Collin County and the town of McKinney – rated at No.1 by *Money Magazine* in 2014 as "Best Place to live in America" – were named in his honour by the Texas legislature in recognition of his contribution to the founding of the Lone Star State.

The second largest city in Collin County, after Plano, and about 32 miles (51km) north of Dallas, McKinney was ranked by the Census Bureau in 2017 as the third fastest-growing in the United States, with a population of close on 192,000.

With its motto 'Unique by nature', and having burgeoned from the 3,000 acres of land on which the original town of the name was built in 1849, it is home to a number of major employers including Raytheon Space and Airborne Systems, while amenities in the city and its environs include the Towne Lake Recreation Area.

Also one of the draftees and signatories in 1836 of the Texas Declaration of Independence from Mexico and a member of the committee that drafted the Constitution of the Republic of Texas, Collin McKinney died in 1861.